How I Saw God Through My Children

How I Saw God Through My Children

Lola Fadipe

Heavenly
Light Press
Alpharetta, GA

ISBN: 978-1-63183-874-3 - Paperback
ISBN: 978-1-63183-875-0 - ePub
ISBN: 978-1-63183-876-7 - Mobi

Library of Congress Control Number: 2020911347

Printed in the United States of America   0 6 2 5 2 0

∞This paper meets the requirements of ANSI/NISO Z39.48-1992 (Permanence of Paper)

First, I give thanks to God for opening my eyes to see Him through a different set of lenses and for the wisdom to relate everyday occurrences with my children to my relationship with Him. I am humbled to be of use in this way. I also want to thank my wonderful husband for his continuous love and support of me. I couldn't have asked for a better partner to journey through life with. Through thick and thin, we have and continue to be friends, partners and lovers. To my children, Sophie and Demi – my very own blessings from God, thank you for being you. For in being you, you've opened my eyes and heart to a better and closer relationship with God.

To my dad, who has gone to be with the Lord, thank you for instilling in me the knowledge that I can do anything. To my mom – thank you for your constant concern for my well-being, prayers, and love for me. To my siblings, thank you for your constant encouragement through the years. I send a special shout-out to my sister Tolani, fondly called Motty – thanks for being the first set of eyes on this book and for your recommendations and continued support.

To my Spiritual mentors Pastors Kunle and Bolaji Akindoju, and Bishop Oluwadipe, thank you for constantly pouring into me and for taking me as one of your own. May you be constantly filled.

To Dione Williams, I don't believe our connection was coincidental, but rather divine. Thank you for being transparent about your struggles and enabling me to take a deeper look at myself. Thank you for connecting me to resources that have aided in the creation of this book.

To all my friends and loved ones, thank you for all the love and support – you know yourselves, and may God's blessings never cease in your lives.

Contents

Preface

This book came about as a result of my personal struggle with trying to understand and receive God's love for me. I always heard growing up that God loved me and even read it too. However, it didn't mean much to me beyond the words – I had the head knowledge that God loved me but didn't comprehend it. How could God, who is all the way in heaven, love little me, in the real sense of love? Don't get me wrong, I fully believed that God gave His Son, Jesus, for my sake, but again, it was merely head knowledge. It was not until I had my kids that I started to relate God's love for me with the way I love my children. It was at that point that I started my journey from head knowledge on this matter, to feeling it in my heart and seeing God's love in my everyday life. I don't use the word "journey" loosely, as I'm still on that path.

My goal and desire from writing this book, is to open my readers' eyes to the same revelation I've had about God. This seeing God from a more relatable perspective will make it easier for people to believe and receive God's love for them. I've chosen to convey these thoughts by sharing simple everyday stories that made an imprint in my heart. I welcome you to come on this journey with me as we see our multi-faceted and amazing God as a father, yes, I said it a father – let that sink in, as we go from knowing that in our head to feeling it in our heart.

Introduction

I'm blessed with two little children. Sophie, my daughter who is 7, and Demi, my son who is 4.

I married in my mid-twenties to the love of my life, who I fondly call Sukkie or Babe. Sukkie and I were together for quite a few years before we got married. I vividly remember when Sukkie and I first met. I was just finishing my shift at McDonald's, where I had worked for a few months. My older sister had come to pick me up, and that day, I was in tears, which for the past few weeks had sadly been a frequent occurrence. I was tired of the job because I had been hired as a cashier but found myself doing everything but making the food. This included cleaning the bathroom stalls, which might not be a big deal for most people, but as a sixteen year old who had lived most of her sheltered life in Nigeria, it was a rude awakening.

I came to the car expecting to see just my sister, but to my surprise, there was a strange guy in the car. I was caught between crying in front of a complete stranger or comforting myself; I chose the former. Sukkie introduced himself, and apparently, he had known my sister back in Nigeria.

We went back to our apartment, and after Sukkie cracked a few jokes, I was no longer crying and soon in a better mood. He asked me why I was crying in the first place, and after explaining my frustrations, he asked a simple question, *"Why don't you quit the job?"* For some reason, I hadn't thought quitting was an option; the thought just hadn't crossed my mind. Although I suspect that if I had, I would have talked myself out of it and found reasons to stay, because I'm not a quitter. It was a huge relief to have an option that would solve all my issues, or at least so I thought. The next day, I quit, but I was asked to come back which I did for a few more days until I was finally done and didn't look back. Now, I'm not a quitter myself, nor am I recommending people become quitters. However, what I learned from this experience was that if something truly makes you unhappy and stressed, sometimes, the solution might be to let it go and that does not make you a quitter. We sometimes have to let go of some things in order to enter into or embrace new things.

The Birth

The day I decided to write this book, I had woken up after a seemingly great night. I had gone out with my husband to a fancy Brazilian steakhouse the night before where we chatted with one of my close friends about some new laws, our views, and people's reactions to these laws. We wrapped up the night early because we were both tired and had work the next day. I was fortunate to work from home on Fridays, however, that morning, I woke up somewhat anxious about things going on at work. I went to my closet to spend some quiet time with God which had become my daily routine. I felt God telling me to take the day off and rest because I was tired, but I made excuses about why I needed to work and how I couldn't cancel my meetings. I asked for the Holy Spirit to strengthen me, which was part of what I was learning through reading Joyce Meyers' books. During this quiet time, I realized I had been putting a lot of pressure on myself and took a moment to put myself in my daughter's shoes seeing her mom put so much pressure on herself. This was the beginning of my journey in seeing God through the eyes of my children. I use the word "journey" intentionally because this has been a series of lessons and experiences which are still ongoing. I decided to write this book to help people see God from a different and more relatable perspective. My hope is that it'll aid in some way to bring the reader closer to God, which is His ultimate desire.

In the following chapters, I'd like you to journey with me through these experiences and what I learned from each of them. Sit back, relax, and enjoy the ride. Be prepared for simple, yet thought-provoking questions. It's important not to feel judged, as that'll completely miss the goal; rather, it's important for us to see through a different pair of eyes which will help us make changes where we need to.

In the beginning was the Word, and the Word was with God, and the Word was God.

—John 1:1 (ESV)

"Truly I tell you, anyone who will not receive the kingdom of God like a little child will never enter it."

—Matthew 18:3 (NIV)

Not everything we want is good for us at the time we want it.

Have you ever considered that not everything we want is good for us at the time we want it? This is especially true when the things we want are good things. Timing is however key; I'm sure you'd agree with me that it's better to get the right things at the right time than to get the right things at the wrong time.

I had been trying to reduce the amount of time my kids spent watching TV because I realized I had been using TV as a distraction to keep the kids busy so that I could have some much needed personal time. Knowing that too much screen time isn't good, I wanted to replace some of the screen time with reading or playing. One Saturday morning, Demi asked to watch TV, and when I said no, he asked to watch on my phone. Again, I said no and asked him to choose between reading his book and playing with his toys. He started throwing a tantrum. I asked him why he was doing that, and he said, "Reading books is boring," and "I don't want to play with my toys." I then told him he would get to watch TV later to which he replied, "Later will take forever." As soon as he said that, it made me think of moments when we pray for something and start throwing tantrums when we don't get an immediate response. We assume God is saying no, but He is actually saying He'll give it to us later and not now.

What Demi did not understand was that I didn't have an issue with him watching TV; however, the timing was important. Had he simply obeyed; he would have gotten to watch TV later. In what ways are we being disobedient to God or assuming God's answer is no when all He wants is the perfect time to give us what we're asking for?

*"Yet the **Lord** longs to be gracious to you; therefore He will rise up to show you compassion. For the **Lord** is a **God** of justice. Blessed are all who **wait** for him!"*
—Isaiah 30:18 (NIV)

Giving Back to God

Isn't it interesting and somewhat painful when we give things to our loved ones and then ask for a portion of it back. Suddenly, they develop an attitude and either refuse to return it, or when they decide to share, they do so grudgingly?

Recently, my son Demi received some gummy bears and jelly beans from school. He asked if he could eat them to which I replied that he should share some with his sister. Sophie took the bag, picked out the biggest gummy bear and a few jelly beans, and then gave the bag back to Demi. Demi said he wanted the biggest gummy bear that Sophie had taken so I asked Sophie to give it to him, and she said, "But I took it first." I said to her, "But it's his, he has chosen to share with you. Why don't you ask Demi if he wants to split it with you?" Grudgingly, Demi agreed to split the gummy bear. Sophie splits it but gives Demi the smaller piece.

Everything we receive comes from God, but sometimes, we find it hard to give back to Him the very things He gave to us. I'm sure a lot of us can see ourselves in Sophie's actions. Often, feelings of entitlement and thinking of ourselves first arise within our hearts.

Everything comes from the Lord. All things were made because of him and will return to him. Praise the Lord forever! Amen.
—Romans 11:36 (CEV)

"But who am I and who are my people that we should be able to offer as generously as this? For all things come from You, and from Your hand we have given You."
—1 Chronicles 29:14 (NASB)

Good Morning

Don't you love it when your loved ones wake up and say good morning to you? How would you feel if they woke up each morning and the first thing they did was start complaining or just jump into conversations about the day without a simple hi, hello, or good morning. Very simple words, but they go a long way and sort of set the tone for the entire day, don't they? In the same breath, it's comforting to know that even when the good morning isn't forthcoming at the time or in the way we'd like it to, we don't stop loving them.

Sophie woke up one morning and rushed up to my room all excited. Her excitement made me excited too. It made me think about how God feels when we wake up in the morning exceedingly excited to be in His presence or even just say good morning to Him.

Demi woke up the same morning, burst into my room, and started talking about Sophie having her bath. Sophie and I sat staring at him, waiting for him to say good morning. Sophie said to him, "Demi, are you forgetting something?" Demi's demeanor expressed an unspoken *what?*. Sophie says, "You haven't said good morning to Mummy." It was funny how Sophie and I both happened to think the same thing (the fact that Demi hadn't greeted and immediately started off with discussing the activities for the day). It was also interesting how different their approaches to saying good morning were. What's more interesting is that even though I preferred Sophie's approach, I embraced Demi when he said good morning. It made me realize God's love for us is without limit, and even when we do things that may not please Him, He still loves us. We don't stop loving our kids when they behave naughty, so why should God stop loving us when we don't act right? This is not to say we should continue in that behavior, but I do think that knowing you are loved regardless of what you do or have done is redeeming.

O Lord, in the morning you hear my voice; in the morning I prepare a sacrifice for you and watch.

—Psalm 5:3 (ESV)

So now there is no condemnation for those who belong to Christ Jesus.

—Romans 8:1 (NLT)

Handling Disappointments

Have you ever thought about how you handle disappointments? By definition, disappointments are setbacks we encounter, and when they happen to us, they don't feel good. Often, we are expecting a certain outcome which with the setback leaves us hanging. The important thing, however, is how we handle these disappointments. While it's important for us to process our feelings, we need to ensure we don't dwell in those feelings, as dwelling in them will extend the disappointment and a longer process to figure the next course of action to achieve what we wanted in the first place.

On one occasion, we had told the kids we were going to Candytopia, a candy show, and you can imagine how excited they were. It was one of the first things they asked for when they woke up that morning and kept asking to go throughout the day. We had planned to go with some family friends, only to find out there were no tickets available. My husband called to see if there was any way to get tickets that day, but not only were there no tickets for the day, there were none available for the entire week. For a child, that was heartbreaking, and even though we told them we would go the following week, to them it seemed like forever. Sophie burst out in tears which made me feel compassionate to her despair. I have been in similar situations, and that it does not feel good when you have your mind set on something and it doesn't happen. The good thing was she was a good sport. She cried hard, but after some consolation, she wiped her tears and started working on her workbook. As a mom, I felt great joy in the fact that she could switch her attitude so quickly and not stay sobbing about something she couldn't change. It made me think about how God wants us to handle situations in a similar fashion. It is okay for us to cry or feel disappointed, but it is also important to not remain in that state. Sometimes, we need to pick ourselves up and change our focus from the disappointing situation.

And we know that for those who love God all things work together for good, for those who are called according to his purpose.

—Romans 8:28 (ESV)

Why are you cast down, O my soul, and why are you in turmoil within me? Hope in God; for I shall again praise him, my salvation and my God.

—Psalm 42:11 (ESV)

Persistency

Have you ever persistently asked for something, and upon receiving it, you were glad you didn't stop? Or do you stop asking because you feel you've asked numerous times and the response hasn't changed?

Children are very persistent, or at least mine are. Sometimes, I give in to requests that I have repeatedly said no to without even realizing it. Other times, I give in for the sake of my peace of mind and choosing my battles. I remember my son one time asking me for permission to watch TV and informing me that his sister had watched one more episode than he had. He did not stop asking me to intervene, which I did, because I got tired of hearing the same request. Another day, my daughter had one helping of ice cream and wanted another. She asked, "Mummy, what would you say if I asked for another helping?" and I replied, "I would say you've had enough." She laughed and asked the same question again, and I gave the same response. She then said she would not stop asking until I gave her more. I thought she was funny and told myself I won't give in. Let's just say after hearing "Mummy, can I have some more ice-cream?" for what felt like forever, not only did I give in, but I also gave her more than one scoop. I also gave her brother some extra as soon as he asked. Interestingly, when she said she would not stop asking, I told myself I would test out the concept of persistence and had truly set my mind on not giving in. This experience has made me a believer in the power of persistence in our requests. If only we, as adults, can be as persistent when asking God for things we desire. To truly incorporate this concept of not letting him rest until He blesses us. The story of Jacob when he fought with the angel comes to mind. Jacob fought with the angel all night and refused to let the angel go until the angel blessed him. It was at that point that his name was changed from Jacob (supplanter) to Israel (contender with God). How many things have we not received, even when working with humans, because we were not persistent? Food for thought.

Then he said, "Let me go, for the day has broken." But Jacob said, "I will not let you go unless you bless me."
—Genesis 32:26 (ESV)

"I tell you, even though he will not get up and give him anything because he is his friend, yet because of his persistence he will get up and give him as much as he needs."
—Luke 11:8 (NASB)

Receiving a "No"

How many times have you said "no" when asked for a request? Or better yet – how many times have you been told "no" when you ask for something? What is your reaction?

If I could get a dollar for the number of times I've said "no" to my children, my pockets would be quite full. But does that stop them from asking? Absolutely not. They ask again for the same thing or something else as if the "no" was an invitation to continue bargaining. Their boldness alone at times makes me give in, especially in instances when I naturally would not have. Why then do we translate a "no" or "not now" from God to mean "I can't trust You, Lord" or "I'm not asking again." I have often heard that we should keep asking until something happens. I can tell you that it is not easy, but if you really want it, you will keep asking until you receive it or you negotiate for something else. If our little children can do it, why not us?

For nothing will be impossible with God."
—Luke 1:37 (ESV)

I waited patiently for the LORD; And He inclined to me and heard my cry.
—Psalm 40:1 (NASB)

Giving
without Expectations

In any relationship, reciprocity or exchanging things equally is important. For some reason, we tend to give more to people in need, often forgetting those we perceive have enough, forgetting that everyone, both rich and poor, the haves and the have nots, have something in common: the desire to be loved and valued by others. Love is not simply just giving, but it is an important part in demonstrating your love. I once heard a wise man say, "You can give without loving, but you cannot love without giving." Just like our Heavenly Father gives to us all the time, he also loves it when we give back to him, without expecting something in return. Giving can be in the form of praise, showing love to others, and much more. My daughter did something simple the other day. She picked up my plate and took it to the kitchen, without me asking. This touched my heart, more than words could tell. I found myself asking my husband to reward this kind act by giving her the iPad to play with, which had been seized a short while before. I did this, simply because her little gesture blessed my heart.

Again, the key or lesson here is not expecting something in return, but doing out of a heart of love.

The point is this: whoever sows sparingly will also reap sparingly, and whoever sows bountifully will also reap bountifully. Each one must give as he has decided in his heart, not reluctantly or under compulsion, for God loves a cheerful giver.

—2 Corinthians 9:6-7 (ESV)

But love your enemies, and do good, and lend, expecting nothing in return, and your reward will be great, and you will be sons of the Most High, for he is kind to the ungrateful and the evil.

—Luke 6:35 (ESV)

Sometimes He Needs People to Help You

Do you know that God needs people to be His hands and feet? Are you like me thinking God works only through miraculous acts? I've come to find He is at work in our everyday life, working through people to bring blessings to us. Be intentional about seeing Him in people around you, and you'll see Him working through everyday people to display His interest in our lives even in the seemingly mundane and simple things.

One lovely Saturday evening, the night after my daughter had won an award in a talent show at her school, I wanted to celebrate with some ice cream, but did not want to promise her because I knew I would not hear the last of it. I also wanted my husband to be part of it so we could have some family time. Earlier that day, I had bought groceries and picked up some cups of ice cream, just in case we were not able to make it to the ice cream shop as I hoped. My daughter asked me for the ice cream in the freezer, and I told her I'd think about it. I said this knowing I had bigger plans (a fancy ice cream shop instead of store-bought ice cream) but needed my husband on board to make it happen. It just made me think about how we pray to God for things, but God is waiting for the person he has sent to be the answer to that prayer to take action. In this case, my husband was part of that answer. Thankfully, he agreed to go, and we were able to kill two birds with one stone: we enjoyed family time and also got to enjoy my daughter's success.

Food for thought: Whose blessings are you holding on to, because you haven't heeded God's nudge?

Contribute to the needs of the saints and seek to show hospitality.

—Romans 12:13 (ESV)

For it is God who works in you, both to will and to work for his good pleasure.

—Philippians 2:13 (ESV)

We Struggle with Him When He Is Trying To Help.

One day, I was asked to help babysit my friend's four-month-old baby who, at the time, was teething. Those who have seen babies' teething process would know it is quite uncomfortable for babies. It hurts so they try to soothe it by sucking on anything nearby including their hands or other objects. This wonderful day, after we had tried a few soothing options: her hands (which she ended up gagging on), her teething toys (didn't seem to do the trick that day), and finally, my own hand, which ended being the longest soothing object. I could tell she was in pain and wanted some relief. She was trying to get my hand into her mouth so she could bite on it which is not as painful as it sounds, since she didn't exactly have teeth yet. Anyways, I sought to offer some relief, but the more I tried to get my hand in her mouth, the more she struggled with me. It just made me think of how we sometimes struggle with God when He is trying to help us, and we act as if we know best how to overcome our struggles. Can you think of times you have done that? Perhaps, He has tried to change a flaw in you or help you navigate something you have failed at multiple times. The good news is she finally allowed me to put my finger in her mouth which helped soothe her gums, and for the germaphobes, I had washed my hands thoroughly before putting it in her mouth. I hope we all do better with yielding to God when He tries to help us. Say this prayer: *Lord, I may not always know when you are trying to help me; help me accept your help without struggling to have my way.*

"For I know the plans I have for you," declares the LORD, "plans to prosper you and not to harm you, plans to give you hope and a future."
—Jeremiah 29:11 (NIV)

For we do not wrestle against flesh and blood, but against the rulers, against the authorities, against the cosmic powers over this present darkness, against the spiritual forces of evil in the heavenly places.
—Ephesians 6:12 (ESV)

A Little Patience?

If you're like me, you want immediate answers to your prayers, especially in this microwave world we live in where immediate gratification is the order of the day. I was hanging out with Demi one day, and the following conversation ensued:

Demi: *"Can I watch TV?"*

Me: *"Later."*

Demi: *"But later is too long."*

Me: *"Do you know when later is?"*

Demi: Getting upset..."*Too long.*"

Me: "Come here," giving him a hug, *"I haven't said 'no,' all I've said is 'later.'"*

Demi: Still upset, *"I know what later is. It is two minutes and half an hour."*

Me: I burst out laughing.

Although I found his comment funny, I didn't see the need for him getting upset, especially since I could out-rightly have said no. A little patience and the right attitude would have gone a long way. I see myself in the way Demi interacted with me that day. Is God telling you later and you're translating that into "no" or throwing an adult tantrum?

Do not be anxious about anything, but in every situation, by prayer and petition, with thanksgiving, present your requests to God.

—Philippians 4:6 (NIV)

Walking with Him

At the beginning of spring, my husband, children, and I went hiking one day in the mountains not too far from our house. The weather was a bit cold so we had to dress warmly. In the past when going on walks as a family, we had to take a stroller for Demi. He was a bit older this time so we didn't take a stroller with us. I was certain he was going to be the one holding us up, based on past experiences. To my surprise, he walked alongside his dad and was way ahead of Sophie and I. Not only was he way ahead, he also went to the top of the second mountain, while Sophie and I stayed behind after the first mountain. What I learned was that by ourselves, we may be weak and only able to go so far, but when we walk alongside God, we are able to go farther than what we or other people think.

Will you choose to walk alongside God today and see how far He'll take you? It may not be an easy journey, but it'll be well worth it.

"You shall walk in all the way that the Lord your God has commanded you, that you may live, and that it may go well with you, and that you may live long in the land that you shall possess."
—Deuteronomy 5:33 (ESV)

Growth

God really wants us to grow, and sometimes, this growth comes about from the challenges he sends our way. For the longest time, I thought that God's love for me meant that I did not have to go through challenges. To be honest, it's something I still battle with even now. I especially struggle with it when I've prayed about it and the challenge still remains.

I remember teaching my four-year-old son how to put his clothes on. I would help him when I saw he was really struggling, but other times, I would let him struggle with it. One particular day, he had put on his shirt with some help from me and also wanted my help putting on his pants. I knew he could do it himself, so even though he asked for my help, I encouraged him to struggle a little until he put it on. I realized that if I kept helping him, he could possibly never see the need to do it himself or even learn to do it himself. To him, it may have seemed unkind of me to be able to help him and yet choose not to, but in reality, it was because I loved him that I chose not to help him. I did this so he could not only learn, but see strength in himself.

Do you think God does not love you because you face challenges? Try to think about it differently. What if He just needs you to learn something? The next time you face a challenge, try asking God what He wants you to learn from it instead of questioning His love for you. It may be a process for you to go from questioning to believing His love, but keep practicing and before you know it, you will truly believe His love for you.

Like newborn babies, crave pure spiritual milk, so that by it you may grow up in your salvation.

—1 Peter 2:2 (NIV)

Say "Yes to Everything" Challenge

"Oh man! How I wish Mummy would do the say yes to everything I ask for one whole day challenge." Those were the words my daughter said to me one day when I said "no" to something she asked for. Now I do not recall what she was asking for; however, her words made me laugh. I was just thinking how wild her asks would be if I agreed to say yes to everything she asked for in a 24-hour period. I also thought it was funny because sometimes I too wonder why everything is not going the way I like. Then, I subsequently start to think that because things are not going my way, God does not love me. How silly I was to think that. I realized it was silly when I thought of how ridiculous it would be if my daughter thought the same of me. The reason why I do not say "yes" to all her demands is because I love her, and I want to prepare her for life when she won't always have her way. My refusal of some of her requests had nothing to do with how much I loved her.

"For I know the plans I have for you," declares the LORD, "plans to prosper you and not to harm you, plans to give you hope and a future."

—Jeremiah 29:11 (NIV)

The LORD appeared to us in the past, saying: "I have loved you with an everlasting love; I have drawn you with unfailing kindness."

—Jeremiah 31:3 (NIV)

Oh,
It's So Hard

Demi can be quite an interesting character. When he does not want to do something, he says "It's too hard" as if saying those words translate to an automatic, "You don't have to do it" or "It's okay to stop." He was swimming the other day, and his swimming instructor had asked him to swim on his back. For some reason, he didn't like doing the backstroke at the time so he said to her, "It's too hard." She said to him with a smile, "It's not hard; you're doing it." Isn't that something we sometimes do when something is hard? One of the ways we can make it easier is by doing it repeatedly. Sometimes, we just want our problems to go away when all we need to do is be patient with ourselves and stay the course until that "hard" thing becomes easy. This is all relative and depends on the circumstances surrounding your situation. Sometimes, the lesson we need to learn is how to realize our strengths in those hardships or getting better at doing that so-called "hard" thing, until it becomes easy. What is that "hard" thing in your life that you know is good for you to do? Is it eating healthy, exercising regularly, or spending time with God?

Demi attends a Christian school and recently graduated from Pre-K. The week of his graduation, they had a recital which I attended. I got there slightly late (which is a story for another day), and as soon as I spotted my son in the midst of other singing kids, my heart lit up. I noticed he was not exactly following the hand movements like the other children and was even yawning at some point, but I didn't care. I realized I was proud of him regardless. He did not need to be perfect for me to be proud of him or to love him. I loved him regardless. That was really refreshing to me, as I have been in the process of believing God loves me, not because of my perfection, which I am not, but in my imperfect state. People have often told me that I do not have to do anything to earn God's love. I never really believed it, but that day, watching my son even in his seemingly imperfection, I got it. It all made sense. If I, a human, love my kids not because of what they do, why would God Almighty require actions in exchange for love? Now, this doesn't mean that our actions do not bring pleasure (or displeasure) to God, but this realization is another step on the journey of receiving and accepting God's unconditional love for me.

Three times I pleaded with the Lord about this, that it should leave me. But he said to me, "My grace is sufficient for you, for my power is made perfect in weakness." Therefore I will boast

*all the more gladly of my weaknesses, so that the power of
Christ may rest upon me. For the sake of Christ, then, I am
content with weaknesses, insults, hardships, persecutions, and
calamities. For when I am weak, then I am strong.*
—2 Corinthians 12:8-10 (ESV)

*Count it all joy, my brothers, when you meet trials of various
kinds, for you know that the testing of your faith produces
steadfastness. And let steadfastness have its full effect, that
you may be perfect and complete, lacking in nothing.*
—James 1:2-4 (ESV)

Reflection
(Made in His Image)

God loves it when we look like him and reflect his goodness. My daughter and I dressed somewhat similar today; we each wore peach dresses that had flowers on them. Although the dresses were not exactly the same, they were similar enough for people to give us compliments about being dressed alike. I call them compliments because it made me happy that people thought we looked alike. I noticed the same smile on my daughter's face. Oh, how it must delight God when we look like and reflect His love for the world to see.

*He is the image of the invisible God, the **firstborn** of all creation.*
—Colossians 1:15 (ESV)

Simple Obedience

God wants us to simply obey him, sometimes without asking questions. We occasionally get into the habit of asking questions when we just need to do what we are asked. This does not mean that asking questions is wrong, but we need to identify the right time to ask them. Being asked to stop when you are about to drive into oncoming traffic is not the right time to ask questions, and while that is an extreme example, it's intended to drive the point home. I know I get frustrated sometimes when I ask my children to do something, and instead of doing it, they resort to asking questions especially when those questions can be asked after they have been obedient. One time, I told Demi to strap on his seatbelt, but he didn't. He instead wanted me to give him my phone and asked if I would give it to him after he was strapped in his seat. The ideal thing for him to do would have been to obey first and then ask for my phone versus asking for my phone as a reward for his obedience.

He replied, "Blessed rather are those who hear the word of God and obey it."

—Luke 11:28 (NIV)

Walk in obedience to all that the Lord your God has commanded you, so that you may live and prosper and prolong your days in the land that you will possess.

—Deuteronomy 5:33 (NIV)

My Tools
vs. Your Tools

God wants us to use our own skills or tools because what works for others may not work for us.

We were finally going on a family trip and those who know me, know that I looooove traveling, especially for pleasure. We were going to Canada, and this happened to be my son's first international trip. I was positively tickled by my son's excitement that I coined the trip "Demi goes to Canada." He was excited about the escalators, the train, his new four-wheel dinosaur suitcase, and just about everything else. His suitcase was easily the same height as him with the handle pulled all the way up, and he insisted on carrying it himself. After all, it was his new suitcase. My daughter's suitcase with Frozen characters on it had only two wheels so it had to be slanted in order to be dragged along conveniently. My son decided to copy her, and we kept telling him that since his suitcase had four wheels, he didn't need to have it slanted at all. In fact, it appeared it would have been easier for him to pull without slanting it. He listened to us and held it upright, and boy, did he struggle because of the height of it. As we walked, my husband and daughter were way ahead of us, so I tried to be patient and let him struggle with the suitcase as he insisted on dragging it himself. After having my husband and daughter wait for us a couple times, I finally decided that maybe he should try slanting the suitcase after all. Wow! It was like night and day. By dragging it that way, he was able to keep pace with the rest of us. Right there, I realized God wants us to use the tools that work for us, not the tools that seem to work for others. The story of David and Goliath comes to mind. David chose to use the tools he was familiar with, which were a sling and stones, instead of using the armor given to him by the king. What tools of others are you holding on to and struggling with? Let go and start using the tools that God has given you.

For more on the story of David and Goliath, read: 1 Samuel 17.

Transitioning

Soon came the time that we had outgrown our town-home; it was the house my husband had bought before our wedding. We had made lots of memories there including the early years of the lives of our two wonderful children. It was a cozy two-bedroom house with a finished base-ment which also had a bedroom, so technically a three-bedroom townhome. We knew we had outgrown the house when my daughter started sleeping in the living room because the only other bedroom on the top floor also housed my son and mother-in-law, who was staying with us at the time. I would see my daughter sleeping on the couch and fight back tears. I was beyond ready to move to a new house. A few years prior, we had started searching for a new house - new construction to be precise. We had gone through dozens of homes, filled with highs and lows. Highs being what could be and lows being what we could realistically afford. Many times I thought we had found the perfect house with enough bells and whistles within our price range, only to have my dreams shattered when my husband had said we were not going to be moving forward. This was particularly disappointing to me because there didn't seem to be a good reason for not buying that home, but it was clear this was his final decision. It actually turned out to be the right one because a few months later he lost his job. It was clear that the house would have been a huge burden on us financially if we had gone forward with the purchase. Fast forward a few years, we started looking again, this time, we went from looking for a house to build, to looking for a house to buy, to looking at apartments, and everything in between. Needless to say, the following weeks were incredibly frustrating with parts that felt like *déjà vu* from our first home search. The real sense of *déjà vu* came when we once again wanted to purchase a house and everything seemed to be in place until it was time to sign the contract, and once again, my husband chose to stop us from moving forward. I shed tears and frankly did not know where to place my frustrations. I could not understand why he would let me fall in love with all these nice homes and then pull the rug right out from under me, especially since we had been down this road before. What could the lesson have been that I didn't learn the first time? And why did it have to be so hard to make a decision and find a home? I was a real estate agent after all, and how ironic it would be if I was helping others find their homes but could not find one of my own. I was celebrating home ownership with others but had to go back to a house that I was grateful for only because I knew I had to be grateful.

Faith Packing

We had started "faith packing." Yes, I said it - faith packing - meaning we did not have a home to move to, but we knew we were moving. I had hoped that this act of faith in itself would open doors and make for an awesome story of faith to reality. I can say that it did end up that way, but the process was not fun at all. My house looked like it had been hit by a hurricane. We would go to work, only to come back, go house hunting, or pack things into boxes. I was ashamed to tell people that we were "faith packing," but I could not think of a more suitable phrase. During that time, we almost signed a contract on a new construction. We had gone there multiple times, took the family there for their approval, went through all the calculations, and all that was left was to obtain signatures and initial payment. We also almost signed a couple leases for rental homes and apartments. However, we ran into issues every time including the process of paying a rental reservation fee, lack for responsiveness, and random excuses from the landlords. We also realized that an apartment would not work for us. As part of my act of faith, I had even selected a four-day long holiday weekend as our move-in time so that I would not have to take additional time off work because of another planned family trip. That long weekend, my hubby and I ended up helping my sister and her family move. It was a bitter-sweet experience, but I'm glad I did not spend the whole time sulking. I was able to find it within me to help someone else with something I myself was looking to God for. This was not easy for me, and I will admit that I cried a bit, but I rallied in the end. This experience gave a new meaning to rejoicing with those who rejoice. Oh, did I mention that in between all of this, my husband and I decided to fast for a full week, seeking God's face after we realized we had jumped into the process without Him. I thought once the fast was over someone would knock on my door and offer me keys to my home - talk about a house delivered straight from heaven. Let's just say that after the fast was over there was no knock on the door. This totally added to my frustration. How could all this time and effort be put into an activity that people do daily without including God and all seems to go smoothly for them? With my limited vision, I couldn't see God at work. As I write this chapter, it's been three days since we received the key to our rental home. It does not have all the bells and whistles like the other homes we had checked out, but it's one I'm grateful for and not grateful because I need to be, but because I truly am.

Sophie has her own room and no longer needs to sleep in the living room. Demi also has his room as well.

I'd be dishonest if I said I would not have preferred one of the nicer ones we looked at, but I trust that there is something better ahead of us. To tell you how radical I was during this process - not sure if it was faith or just really wild imaginations, I went to check out a property that was almost $1.5M. My husband joked that even if both our salaries and income were combined we would not come close to being considered. The future will tell where the line is between faith and imagination. When God said nothing is impossible for Him, I assumed that included the $1.5M home.

In the same way, faith by itself, if it is not accompanied by action, is dead.

—James 2:17 (NIV)

For we live by faith, not by sight.

—2 Corinthians 5:7 (NIV)

God Wants Us to Trust Him More

During one of our family vacations, we took a train to one of our destinations. It was the first time the children had been on a train or at least the first time they were aware of being on one. We had just finished touristy activities at the CN tower. The kids and I were hungry so we had brought some snacks with us because we knew the food at the tourist attractions would be expensive. The children had picked their favorite bags of chips to hold them over during the train ride, and I had picked a bag of granola balls. My husband and I helped ourselves to their chips, and then I opened my bag of granola balls. It tasted really good but didn't have the crunch I had anticipated. I offered my daughter a ball to taste; I did not want her wasting it if it turned out she did not like it. After tasting it, she told me, "It's so yummy" and then said, "Mummy, can I have two more?" I knew she wanted more than two, but only asked for two because she assumed it was an amount that would not make her seem greedy and a quantity I could easily part with. I ended up giving her double what she asked for and would have given her even more if she had asked. How many times have you shortchanged yourself by asking God for less than you truly wanted or desired? At the end of the day, the responses you'll hear are yes, no, or later. Any of those would be better than if we never asked. As if to validate this chapter, not even a minute after I thought I was done with this chapter, my daughter asked for more granola balls, and this time, she asked for "more" instead of a specific count. This time, I handed her the whole bag.

Being Content with God's Blessings

Have you ever looked at someone and wondered why they have so much more than you? Or do they have the very things you crave? And then you wonder why God blessed them with those things and not you. That was me. I had been feeling this way for a few days. I knew we are supposed to be content with what we have, but that day, I was not quite feeling very content. In fact, I had to pray and then talk myself out of my mood. We were on vacation at the time, and for some reason, I could not snap out of this mood, nor could I put a finger on what exactly was wrong. I did not like the feeling and was even more upset at my behavior. Thankfully in time, I was able to snap out of it with the help of the Holy Spirit. Then we all started having fun; we were out with the children participating in tourist activities. After we finished, we picked up a few souvenirs. My son picked a pair of sunglasses and a hat; he wanted to match with his dad. My daughter picked a pair of sunglasses, since hers had gotten lost during the trip. She also picked up a mood necklace and a keychain that had her name on it. We left the store, and they each started putting on the items we had purchased, when my son started whining that he only had two items. It was then it dawned on me, how God must feel when He gives us what He feels is right for us at the time, and we act un-appreciative. It also made me realize that there is no way we would be happy if He gave us all the same exact things. It would not only take away from what makes us unique, but if we were to apply it to material things, it could be inappropriate in some situations. For example, imagine if I gave my son the same purple sunglasses my daughter had picked that said "girl power." He is not a girl, and purple is not one of his favorite colors. The point is we are all unique in our own ways, and God blesses us by treating us as individuals.

Egg Explosion

I was getting ready for a women's conference and running late but had to make breakfast for my children. I was rushing around and a bit disheveled. The waffles had been popped in the toaster, and I was rinsing some grapes while trying to get their plates and cups set up. As a super multi-tasker, or so I thought, I decided to put a pre-boiled egg from the fridge into the microwave for a few seconds. I set it for thirty seconds with the intent of turning off half-way through. Instead of focusing my time on waiting for the egg to get warm enough and then turning off the microwave, I decided to do a couple other things to save time. While doing those things, I heard an explosion and immediately knew what it was. The boiled egg had exploded. My immediate thoughts were "Oh No!" "Why me," and "Why today of all days." My husband is very neat, and I knew I could not leave the egg in the microwave like that simply because I was in a hurry. For anyone who this has happened to, you know it is not exactly easy to clean. You literally have to clean the entire microwave, including all the creases you did not know a microwave had. It dawned on me - I was now spending five minutes cleaning a mess that could have been avoided if I had focused for just fifteen seconds. Needless to say, I learned my lesson this time, and sad to say, this had not been my first time round the egg explosion rodeo, but it turned out to be the most impressionable and memorable. You may ask, why all this rambling about an exploded egg? There is a lesson in this; it is the small and seemingly inconsequential events in life that can teach us the biggest lessons, with the smallest consequences. If I find a challenging task at work, do you think I now focus my attention on this in order to avoid potentially wasting additional time and resources fixing a mistake caused by multitasking? Absolutely!!! God wants us to learn from our little mistakes and avoid making ones on a larger scale.

Let your eyes look straight ahead; fix your gaze directly before you.
—Proverbs 4:25 (NIV)

The steadfast of mind You will keep in perfect peace, Because he trusts in You.
—Isaiah 26:3 (NASB)

Teeth Brushing Fiasco

We had just gotten back from our family connect night. It's a night where our whole family does an activity together. That night, the activity involved getting ice cream and some really good pizza. We were in line for an ungodly amount of time, but that is a story for another day. Long story short, it was a nice outing and one that was really timely too. I had a horrible day earlier which made me want the ground to swallow me, and I was feeling tired of life's little frustrations and trapped. By the end of the evening, I was feeling more like myself again and even felt up to going shopping for groceries on our way home. A very simple activity on a normal day, but certainly a victory on this given day. Later than evening, I was brushing my son's teeth when he asked why his sister got two things and he only got one. You see, at the grocery store, we split ourselves into two groups; my daughter went with my husband and my son with me. The plan was to divide and conquer. My daughter kept asking my husband to buy her a few things, and he kept saying, "No," until he gave in and allowed her to pick up a chocolate that had two bars in the pack. There is something to be said about persistence. When we regrouped at the checkout lane, she asked me to buy her a candy box that had a toy; I gave in because she mentioned that would be her reward for getting recognized for good behavior that week at school. That was cheaper than what I had originally planned to get her, so I delightfully said yes to the idea of keeping a few more dollars in my pocket. I had gotten my son some socks during this shopping trip, and this was the *one* item he was referring to. I immediately asked him to stop comparing and told him that he had a different name from his sister and should not always expect to have the same things. It made me realize how God must feel each time we compare ourselves to others. If we actually counted what my son got that night, it would have been more than what my daughter had gotten. The socks, which had six pairs in the pack, also cost more than the chocolate and candy; plus, my daughter had been instructed to give him one of the bars once she opened it. I explained this to him and made sure he understood why comparing was wrong. He reluctantly agreed, which can't always be expected from a five-year-old.

Do we compare ourselves with others, or compare the God-given talents in others to ourselves? Besides the fact that comparing is wrong, do you know that our comparisons are never comparing apples with apples? We never compare the same things with each other because in the first place, none of us are created the same, nor are our life journeys the same. Let's try practicing appreciation for the gifts in others and thanksgiving for the gifts in us, instead of comparing.

Each of you must examine your own actions. Then you can be proud of your own accomplishments without comparing yourself to others. Assume your own responsibility.
—Galatians 6:4-5 (GW)

The man said, "Let me go; it's daybreak." Jacob said, "I'm not letting you go 'til you bless me."
—Romans 12:6a (MSG)

Attitude in Making Requests

It was Saturday morning, and our family routine was for the kids to come to our bedroom and hang out for a bit. Depending on how tired we were, they would sleep with us, or we would all start playing and then pray. That Saturday morning, my husband had gone out for a meeting so it was just me in bed by the time the kids made their rounds. They had slept for a bit and played with each other, while I was trying to get the last few minutes of my beauty rest. My daughter asked if she could watch videos on my phone, and I said, "No." Then she politely asked if she could watch TV to which I answered, "Yes." My son on the other hand started grumbling and asked if he could use my phone. He asked without using the "magic" word, "please," so I blurted out, "No!" He asked why, and I told him it was because of his attitude. He got off the bed and went into my bathroom throwing a mini tantrum. I had already learned long ago to ignore these tantrums. Before long, he came back and asked very nicely with no sign that he had just been naughty, so I said, "Yes." And I said to him, "Do you see how much difference a good attitude made?" It is that easy with God too. Are we going to Him with bad attitudes and expecting a "yes" response? I am guilty of this. Let us approach Him with the right attitude, just like we would like others to approach us when they need something from us.

Humble yourselves before the Lord, and he will exalt you.
—James 4:10 (ESV)

Do not be anxious about anything, but in everything by prayer and supplication with thanksgiving let your requests be made known to God.
—Philippians 4:6 (ESV)

Hope Deferred – Demi's Treat

It is our family tradition to give our kids treats when they do well at school. We would start off with a daily treat based on their daily report from school, and then graduate to a weekly treat once the daily behavior became a habit. At Demi's school, a star meant he was on his best behavior, and a smiley face was the next best thing. I cannot tell you what the other two options were because Demi knew better than to come home with anything less than a smiley face. He had been getting quite a few smiley faces and so we were encouraging him to get that coveted star. In fact, Sophie took it upon herself to find out from Demi's teacher the qualifications for getting a star. A couple weeks into the new school year, Demi got his first star! We were all thrilled, and his treat was ice cream from a great ice cream spot where we had to stand in line for over thirty minutes just to order, but it was all worth it because Demi had gotten his first star. The reward must have worked, because soon after, Demi started coming home with more stars. On this particular day, a Wednesday to be exact, I vividly remember because we were at church for the mid-week service. I had come straight from work, so I met the rest of my family at church. Upon seeing me, the first thing Demi said to me was, "I got a star!" I was excited as usual, and he then proceeded to ask for his treat. I told him I could not give it to him at that time, since we were still at church. Oh boy! What came next was unexpected: he burst into tears and started crying saying that this meant he would not get any treat since we would go home after church and he would be told it was too late to get a treat. I could not address his concerns at the time because service was beginning, and I wanted to listen to the word. Service ended with Demi still in tears. My pastor had seen him and upon finishing the service asked me what was going on. After my explanation, he said since it is a family tradition, Demi was asking for what was rightfully his. I did not have any opposition to this; instead, my position was that I could not give him the treat right there and then. I was also not in the mood to baby him into understanding that point. Luckily for Demi, my pastor gave him a $20 bill, which was more than I could have given him as a treat. Hope deferred can be a challenge to experience, but the end thereof is usually better than we could have ever anticipated.

Hope deferred makes the heart sick, but desire fulfilled is a tree of life.
—Proverbs 13:12 (ESV)

Like cold water to a weary soul, So is good news from a distant land.
—Proverbs 25:25 (NASB)

Joyful Living

I haven't always been the all-smiles type of person. In fact, my mom would tap my head as a child and say in our language, "Stop squeezing your face." This, of course, aggravated me even more. I didn't understand at the time that she was trying to soften my strong, concentrated-looking face. As an adult, I'm still working on breaking this multi-decade habit. Sophie and Demi to my delight have the best smiles. It is easy to tell when they are upset, but other than that, they are the epitome of joyful living. They are constantly bubbly and filled with positive energy, even over the littlest things. I could watch them for hours and just wonder how they manage to be without a care in the world. Even when they are upset, it for such a short time, and they are back to being their bubbly selves. No wonder Jesus said that unless we change and be like children, we won't enter the kingdom of heaven.

I once asked Sophie, "How do you stay so happy?" She said to me, "I think happy thoughts and do things that make me happy." *That simple, huh?* I thought to myself. I do believe that they will remain this joyful even as adults, as it's my constant prayer for them. Sophie's middle name means "God has made joy," and Demi's full name means "God has crowned me with the crown of joy." Their names were selected as a result of personal struggles with depression (story for another day), and my resolve that they would not have such experiences.

You may be wondering, *What does all this have to do with me and joyful living?* Well, everything. You see, God wants us to live in a constant state of joy. He even commanded us to "rejoice always." It brings Him pleasure to see us joyful. I can't fully express with words how I feel when I see my children being so joyful; it refreshes my soul and reminds me not to take life so seriously.

What are ways you can start "rejoicing always"? Perhaps, you can start with your thoughts – thinking happy thoughts and doing the things that make you happy. I recently started attending a dance class in an effort to spend more of my time doing the things I enjoy, and what a difference it has made. It gives me something to look forward to, has increased my confidence, and enables me to let loose and be free. You can do the same thing too – let go of those excuses you've made and start living a life full of joy. Smile more, laugh more, even if it's only because God wants you to.

And he said: "Truly I tell you, unless you change and become like little children, you will never enter the kingdom of heaven."
—Matthew 18:3(NIV)

Rejoice in the Lord always. I will say it again: Rejoice!
—Philippians 4:4 (NIV)

Win-Win Situation

Sophie and Demi have said to me so many times, that I've actually lost count, "Mom, you're the best mom." Those words are gold to me, pure gold. Unbeknownst to them, those words have carried me through some of my darkest days. I can't think of any other words they can say to me that will mean more to me. Those words mean they accept me with all my flaws and still think I'm the best. Over the years, I've learned, and I'm still learning to completely own those words. They bring me comfort, encouragement, and strength; they are a symbol of their satisfaction in me, which causes me to take great pleasure in them and makes me want to do even more for them.

God is the same way. He doesn't want us to just know and obey Him; He wants us to be satisfied, content, and enjoy being with Him. He wants us to delight and take pleasure in Him, and in doing so, He even promises to give us the desires of our hearts. That sounds like a win-win situation to me, and I dare say we have the better end of the deal. Delighting ourselves in God brings us pleasure in itself, but God doesn't just stop there – He extends the benefit to giving us the things that our hearts truly desire.

Delight yourself in the Lord, and he will give you the desires of your heart.

—Psalm 37:4 (ESV)

Mommy and Sophie Time

Sophie, to my pleasure, enjoys hanging out with me. I haven't quite figured out why yet, although I know she does enjoy the benefits like eating out, shopping, etc. If these were the only times she pushed to hang out with me, I'd have said it was only for the benefits she derived from the hangouts. However, she's proven over time that she enjoys time with me, even when there's no apparent benefit (e.g. taking walks, just chilling in my room, etc.). She has taken some interesting steps to protect her "Mommy and Sophie time" as she so eloquently calls it. Some of which have been to my amazement, but ultimately, leads to an all around enjoyable experience. I recall taking her and Demi to play with their nephews one day after church because Sophie had requested to go to their house. However, as soon as we got to the door, she allowed Demi to enter first and then said she no longer wanted to go and that she wanted to hang out with me instead. Mind you – she was pushing for us to go to their house up until this moment. I was completely confused about her changing her mind, until I realized she was pushing for us to go to their house so we could drop Demi off and have our "Mommy and Sophie time." When I realized it, I was both perturbed at her smartness as well as delighted at the lengths she went in order to hang out with me. We ended up having a wonderful time going out to brunch. That day officially started our Sunday brunch tradition, which we do as frequently as time allows.

Imagine how God feels when we set time aside with just Him. How do you spend your "God and you time"? Do you make arrangements and ignore other activities to spend time with Him? If not, you should try it out and don't stop at trying, but make it a routine.

"Draw near to God and He will draw near to you."
—James 4:8 (NASB)

Then you will call upon Me and go and pray to Me, and I will listen to you. And you will seek Me and find Me, when you search for Me with all your heart.
—Jeremiah 29:12-13 (NKJV)

Mercy Mercy

Sophie had done a few naughty things within a short time period. These included taking out part of her braids in the middle of a school week – the braids had taken planning to get done and we were about a week away from when they were to be taken out – to telling white tales, to being unkind to her brother, which is a huge peeve of mine. I love when they are kind to each other instead of being mean to each other. She even managed to ruin some things that her dad and I had worked hard to buy for her. Each time I wanted to discipline her, the word "mercy" came to my mind, and so, I resorted to talking to her about it instead of giving her the discipline I thought she deserved. Don't get me wrong; I'm a strong believer in child discipline, but there are instances that do call for mercy in place of punishment. Mercy means compassion, kindness and or forgiveness shown toward a person, whom it is within one's power to punish or harm. i.e. the punishment is well deserved, but in lieu of punishment, compassion is shown or expressed. It's easier to be on the receiving end of mercy than to be on the giving end. In order to show mercy, some level of restraint and patient thinking are needed. It's important to note that in order to be on the receiving end of mercy, you also need to be on the giving end.

God has shown mercy to us in so many ways and still continues to. Can you imagine what life would be like if we were punished for everything we do that is wrong? This is not to say we don't receive the consequences of our actions; however, I'm thankful when I receive mercy knowing I've been in the wrong. Who has wronged you that you haven't forgiven, who's in need of your mercy today? Choose to show mercy and watch God give it right back to you when you need it the most. Did you know there are roughly 38 verses on mercy in the Bible. This works out to more than one verse about showing mercy for each day of the month.

If you are like me, I grew up thinking God punished us for every single sin we committed. I don't know if this was instilled in me as a child or was a result of an assumption I made. As an adult, I've come to learn that that's not the case. The Bible says "The Lord is gracious and full of compassion, slow to anger and great in mercy. The Lord is good to all, and His tender mercies are over all His works." (Psalm 145:8-9) I hope this is as much of an eye-opener for you as it's been for me. God is not the big bad wolf just waiting to take a bite each time we go wrong.

Lola Fadipe

"Blessed are the merciful, For they shall obtain mercy."
—Matthew 5:7 (NKJV)

Be merciful, even as your Father is merciful.
—Luke 6:36 (ESV)

Changing Strategies

One day, I asked Sophie to assist me with doing the laundry. This was part of me intentionally teaching my children to assist with home chores preparing them for their future. On this day, we had a pile load of laundry, and I needed her help with hanging some of the clothes out to dry. It was winter, and we needed to air dry the sweaters, sweatshirts, and similar clothes to prevent them from shrinking. I asked Sophie to get some hangers from Demi's room which she did. Then I asked her to put some of Demi's clothes on hangers. My plan was to hang them up after she put each one on a hanger. This day, Sophie decided to go the extra mile and wanted to put them up herself. She had successfully put the first one up but seemed to have some trouble putting the second one up. I asked if I could help, and she insisted on handling it herself. I didn't mind at all and admired her persistence, as she jumped multiple times attempting to hang the sweatshirt on the laundry railing. After a few unsuccessful tries, I started wondering if she would ask for help or try something different, since what she was doing didn't seem to be working. A few more tries later, I was just about to tell her I'd help, when she asked me to help her. I was excited because she had decided on a different strategy. I used that as an opportunity to teach her that when we try the same thing multiple times and it doesn't work, sometimes, all we need to do is to change our strategy. I lifted her up and had her hang the sweatshirt herself. We were both happy – I was happy to help her, and she was happy she got to hang the sweatshirt, only with a bit of help and change in strategy.

Have you been trusting God for something and asking the same way with no results? Are there things you've been doing over and over and getting the same result, but expecting a different outcome? You may need to seek God's face to discover what changes you need to make in your unsuccessful strategy. You may need to change it a few times until you get it right; however, don't give up; God doesn't want you to. A simple tweak may be all you need.

"Trust in the Lord with all your heart. Never rely on what you think you know. Remember the Lord in everything you do, and he will show you the right way. Never let yourself think that you are wiser than you are; simply obey the Lord and refuse to do wrong."
—Proverbs 3:5-7 (GNB)

In all your ways acknowledge him, and he will make straight your paths.
—Proverbs 3:6 (ESV)

Little Helper

It was a Friday morning, and Sophie wanted me to join her at school for lunch. I had barely slept the night before and wasn't sure I'd be able to clear my schedule that day to make it, especially since it was a last-minute request. I had been feeling the need to spend quality time with both Sophie and Demi, since my work week had been hectic and had me coming home late. This made me feel the need to make an extra effort to go to her school that day. I had started working early since I couldn't sleep well. Before lunch, I took a break, hopped in the shower, and made my way to her school. I hadn't packed any special lunch, since I had sent her off to school with the lunch I'd prepared the day before. On getting to her school, I checked in and headed right to the breakroom. I was early so her class hadn't made it over yet. I spent the time watching kids come in and out with their classmates and waited eagerly to see Sophie. A few minutes passed and there she was, I spotted her right at the door. I'd spent the previous few minutes running my eyes back and forth across the hall to see if she was already there. Our eyes met, and the pure delight in her eyes was indescribable. She was excited to see me – more so since I didn't confirm that I'd be there. We made our way to a private table and started chit chatting while she ate her lunch. She wanted to invite one of her friends to join us, but I expressed my dislike of this idea as I was barely fully present there myself. She stepped away to go say hello to her friends; if you can't tell, she's a social butterfly. I joyfully watched her interact with her friends while I waited for her to return. I turned to look at my phone for a quick minute and heard a sound, so I looked in the direction of the noise and realized one of her friends had dropped her lunch. I was trying to decipher if Sophie was the one who caused the fall when I saw her bend down to help her friend clean up the spilled food. I was so proud of Sophie's actions. While others stood by and watched, she delved right in and helped. I was both excited that she had learned what I had been teaching her and that she didn't need any coercion or validation from her friends. How proud God must be of us when we help others in need.

Let each of you look not only to his own interests, but also to the interests of others.

—Pilippians 2:4 (ESV)

Do not neglect to do good and to share what you have, for such sacrifices are pleasing to God.

—Hebrews 13:16 (ESV)

But You Gave Sophie and Didn't Give Me...

"But you gave it to Sophie and didn't give me one…" These are my least favorite words to hear Demi say. It makes me cringe each time I hear it, because it is his way of comparing himself to his sister. It comes in different forms – "But Sophie has it, and I don't," "Why did you give that to Sophie and didn't give me one?" or "Sophie has 5, and I got only 3." All of these are said with the infamous whining tone. In fact, I'm not sure which I like less – the tone or the words; let's just go with both.

While they are similar, in that they are both my children, each has completely different personalities, ages, and therefore, maturity levels. This further concerns me each time he compares himself with his sister, especially when he feels he is getting the short end of the stick. It hurts to see him do that, and I wish he'd understand he is a different person and there's no good in comparing himself with anyone. There will always be someone who has more.

This makes me wonder how God must feel seeing us

compare ourselves to others. We are never comparing apples to apples as we are all different. God, more than anyone else, knows our weaknesses and our shortcomings, yet He doesn't compare us to other people He created and doesn't want us comparing ourselves to others. In fact, God says that those of us who compare ourselves with each other are without understanding. Makes perfect sense to me – every time I see Demi comparing himself, it reminds me that he doesn't see himself the way I see him; he doesn't see that there are reasons why he's been given less. Sometimes, it's because of his capacity; other times, it's because he is younger, asked after the fact, or even just a matter of timing of things. However, it is never because he is loved less, even though that's how he seems to interpret it, or that he is being treated unfairly. Next time you want to compare yourself with another person, think about how you'd feel if your child was acting that way, or better still if God was right there watching you.

Not that we dare to classify or compare ourselves with some of those who are commending themselves. But when they measure themselves by one another and compare themselves with one another, they are without understanding.
—2 Corinthians 10:12 (ESV)

You Ordered?

I usually pack school lunches for Sophie and Demi to take to school; it's normally something as simple as the pre-packaged Lunchables and yoghurt or homemade sandwiches – yes, I'm one of those moms. They don't mind buying lunch from the school cafeteria; in fact, before I started packing them, they looked forward to it. My only issue with it was the fact that there was no control over what they ordered; there was a time when Sophie would buy snacks every day, and this was in addition to the snacks I had already packed her. So in order to manage the amount of unhealthy food they ate, I preferred packing their lunch then having them order food at school.

One wonderful morning as they were getting ready for school, Demi wanted to know if he could order lunch at school that day. It so happened that Sophie had seen me packing their lunch the day before and told him they were having chicken nuggets and Oreo cookies. I thought Demi would be excited, since he enjoyed eating chicken nuggets. In fact, that was the only form of chicken he would eat. Alas! He squealed, "But that's what we had for lunch yesterday," and went off whining. At first, I wasn't sure what to say, and I sure wasn't going to change his lunch option because of his outburst. A few minutes later, I couldn't clearly hear the conversation that ensued between Sophie and Demi, but the next thing I heard was, "You ordered lunch?" and Demi's whining got louder… "But Mummy, you didn't let me order lunch yesterday, and you allowed Sophie." It was clear to me that either Sophie had told a fib about being allowed to buy school lunch the day before, or Demi made an assumption she did and wasn't corrected. I was immediately upset at watching Demi go through pain that was triggered by this untruth. I scolded Sophie for telling him she ordered lunch or not correcting his assumption and instead watching him agonize about it.

This made me wonder how God feels when we flaunt our good fortunes or blessings in people's faces. Still on the topic of comparison, while comparison is wrong, I believe it's just as bad when we make people feel the need to compare themselves or don't share with them that the grass isn't as green as they think. I think a lot of us would have been spared much heartache if people were real about their circumstances, instead of deceiving us into believing they have it way better.

But now you are proud and you brag. All of this bragging is wrong. Anyone who knows the right thing to do, but does not do it, is sinning.

—James 4:16-17 (NCV)

Do nothing from selfish ambition or conceit, but in humility count others more significant than yourselves.

—Philippians 2:3 (ESV)

Can I Have
Some Quiet Please?

Anyone who knows Sophie, knows she's a chatterbox. This aspect of her character can sometimes be a blessing and other times, not so much. I'm on my journey to being a morning person, story for another day, which means for the time being the last thing I want to do in the morning is talk. I love to ease into my day with peace and quiet and only speak when necessary or when I'm spending time in prayer. I enjoy Sophie's vibrant attitude more during the day and into the evening. This particular morning, Sophie decided to come into my room in the morning while I was taking a shower; initially, I was startled and thought she just wanted to get something. Well, let's just say that wasn't her plan. It seemed she was initiating another Sophie and Mummy time. I didn't mind her presence much and, in fact, was enjoying it until she started talking and wouldn't stop. She went from asking questions to making unsolicited comments and back to questions again. The questions ranged from why I like wearing makeup to if she could try it out, then comments about my foundation looking orange, and it went on and on for what felt like forever. The individual questions and comments by themselves were ok, in little doses. But imagine getting asked questions back to back with more questions and comments before you even had a chance to answer the last one. Well, let's just say it felt overwhelming. So overwhelming that I had to ask for her to give me my space. I had a few things on my mind before she appeared, and I just couldn't take one more question that morning, because it was beginning to feel like a one direction conversation. *Does* this *sound familiar?* I bet you'd say no. Now, let me help jog your memory. *How do you pray to God? Is it one directional?* I hear some of you responding, of course it is. We sometimes pray to God and don't stop long enough to hear Him speak back to us. The next time you decide to pray, think about how you'd feel if someone literally talked you out of the conversation. *How would you feel?* And will the person get much out of you, most likely not, because they wouldn't even give you the time to hear you out. Let's spend time listening more to God than attempting to outtalk Him. It's a good thing God doesn't get overwhelmed; otherwise, some of us would have worn Him out long ago.

Let's not forget that although He can't be overwhelmed or allows us to talk so much, it doesn't mean He has nothing to say. In fact, He has a lot to say, but only if we stop and listen. I'm guilty of this same thing, but the good news is we can always make progress. Let's do it! We can!!!

*Call to me and I will answer you and tell you great and
unsearchable things you do not know.*
—Jeremiah 33:3 (NIV)

*Jesus answered, "It is written: 'Man shall not live on bread
alone, but on every word that comes from the mouth of God.'"*
—Matthew 4:4 (NIV)

Thank You

Thank You – two words that can change everything. It is a really powerful phrase if you think about it deeply. It has the power to make one feel appreciated, bring smiles to a person's face, cause a person to want to give more, and the list goes on. I love hearing my children use this phrase and love it more when it comes without coercion. To be honest, I'd still take it even when it's coerced and prefer the coerced version to not having it said at all. It's a phrase I learned as a child and has made a difference in my life both from being thankful and receiving gratitude from others.

I remember driving the kids after a school lesson one day. I had stopped by a store to pick up some cookies and couldn't wait to get home to start nibbling on them. I gave each of them one cookie and didn't hear anything for a minute or so. When Sophie decided to speak, it was her telling me she didn't like the cookie. Demi, on the other hand, seemed to love it. I was too focused on the drive that I initially hadn't realized that neither of them said thank you, at least not until Demi asked for another cookie. This time, I decided to give him a different one, he took it, said he preferred it to the first one, and wanted Sophie to try it, so I gave her a piece, as I didn't want her wasting it like she did the first one. She liked it, so I offered her a whole cookie. As the cookie left my hand, I said "You're welcome!" That was my way of reminding them they hadn't said thank you. This prompted Sophie to say, "Thank you, Mummy," and in true fashion, Demi followed suit. Now they didn't stop at saying it just once, it seemed like they got into a thank you competition. The next thing I heard was, "I said it more times than you," and the next few minutes went on with them insisting on how many times each of them said thank you. I just burst out laughing. I didn't mind them saying thank you multiple times, neither did I mind that I had to remind them before they said it.

How many times have you received something from God and forgot to say thank you? Remember the story of the ten lepers? What separated the grateful one from the rest? Gratitude! Let's remember to incorporate gratitude in our relationship with God. Don't save it just for Thanksgiving Day, try incorporating it in your everyday life, and watch your life transform. You will like it, and so will He, in fact, He demands it.

Give thanks in all circumstances; for this is God's will for you in Christ Jesus.

—1 Thessalonians 5:18 (NIV)

Let us come before him with thanksgiving and extol him with music and song. For the LORD is the great God, the great King above all gods.

—Psalm 95:2-3 (NIV)

Just
Ask For Help

Every first Sunday of the month is a Thanksgiving Sunday at our church. Baby dedications, milestone birthday celebrations, etc. are all done on Thanksgiving Sundays. The service is longer, and as it's the beginning of the month, many people, including myself, pay more attention to wearing our Sunday best on that occasion! This Thanksgiving Sunday was no different; Demi's suit had just been dry-cleaned, so I brought it out for him to wear to church. It was a grey suit, and he happened to also have a nice new shirt and shoes his dad bought him a few months before to go with it. He looked really spiffy that day and even received lots of compliments. We got home from church, and it was time for Demi to take off his clothes and change into his pajamas, yes! I didn't have plans on taking him anywhere else and didn't want to waste an extra set of clothes. I helped him take off his jacket and asked him to take off the rest. I was tired and wanted to finish up the necessary household chores and catch a nap. I was barely down the stairs when I heard Demi whining. I couldn't hear him clearly, but from the words I could pick out, it sounded like he was having trouble taking off his belt and pants. Then his voice grew louder, and he went from whining to plain old wailing. At first, I wasn't sure how to react. If I hadn't picked out a few words, I'd have thought he had gotten hurt, or something else was seriously wrong. It wasn't the first time he'd taken off his clothes, and I'd taught him to ask for help when he needed it instead of crying. Let's just say he didn't heed my teaching on this blessed Sunday. I stood at the end of the stairs and asked him what was wrong and why he was crying? Then, I noticed his sister trying to help him. He was so upset that he didn't accept the help, nor could he get out words to explain what was wrong when I asked. I told him to stop crying and accept the help his sister was offering. I again reminded him to always ask for help first.

I'm not sure if the issue is pride or forgetfulness, but many times, we get ourselves upset or frustrated just like this when all we need to do is ask for help. God is willing to help us when we ask for help and the help could come in different forms, through His still, small voice or through another person. It goes without saying that God won't come down to help us; He uses people. The next time you find yourself upset or frustrated, instead of throwing an adult tantrum (I'm a testament that they exist – thankfully, less frequent than in the past), will you ask Him for help?

"Come to me, all you who are weary and burdened, and I will give you rest. Take my yoke upon you and learn from me, for I am gentle and humble in heart, and you will find rest for your souls. For my yoke is easy and my burden is light."
—Matthew 11:28-30 (NIV)

My help comes from the Lord, who made heaven and earth.
—Psalm 121:2 (ESV)

I Love
Them Either Way

Sophie and Demi are by no means perfect children. In fact, they are imperfect, and that's just the way I love them. There are countless times I wish they'd act in certain ways, or as I say to them often, "Simply do the right thing" instead of apologizing after the fact. However, regardless of their actions or inactions, I LOVE them and that will never change. In fact, I dare say there's nothing they can do, or not do, that will make me love them any more or less. My love for them is full. I may like them more or less depending on if they're naughty or nice. I may like what they do more or less depending on their actions, but my love for them remains constant. I've heard it said of God numerous times that His love for us is perfect, and it's sometimes hard for us to comprehend because we measure His love based on our expectations, understanding of love, and sometimes the blessings He gives us or doesn't give us.

Love is not measured in gifts, nor is it measured based on expectations. We don't love our kids more because they do the right thing, nor do we love them less when they don't. *So why do we have a different expectation of God? Why do we find it hard to believe and receive His love for us?* Perhaps, we have translated love to mean something else, or we look at love through the lens of the world. He says His love for us is perfect, and so it is. Even if we don't believe it, it doesn't change that fact. Think about it – *What else can He do for us, that will be a greater expression of love than laying down His son, Jesus, to die for us?* Will that thing that we long for and claim He cannot love us without giving to us, or some tragedy that He allowed to happen blur His love for us? If we're being honest and realistic, nothing can topple the love He has already demonstrated towards us. This means we need to learn to receive His love. It's available to us.

Greater love has no one than this: to lay down one's life for one's friends.
                                        —John 15:13 (NIV)

Whoever does not love does not know God, because God is love.
                                        —1 John 4:8 (NIV)

Who Started It First?

"He started it first!" "No! She started it first!" Whenever I hear those words, I know a dispute has begun between Sophie and Demi, and they are pointing fingers as to who started the fight. As a mom, "who" started it first doesn't matter much. It's the fact that they are fighting in the first place that bothers me. Ultimately, while I try to hear them out in order to settle the dispute, I focus more on the fact that they should be showing each other love and not fighting. My words to them are, "You should be loving each other not fighting each other. You're brother and sister!"

One day is no different than other days when they have a squabble; the only differences are what triggered the squabble, the location, and how high they raised their voices at each other before there's an intervention. It's amazing how siblings, who can be so loving to each other one minute, can start pointing fingers, upset at each other the next minute. They were on the table eating their dinner, and all seemed well and normal. I was taking a short break on the living room couch when I heard them yelling at each other. Initially, I didn't want to engage – I wanted them to resolve the issue on their own. When I realized their voices were only getting louder, I told them to stop it. Notice – I didn't ask for an explanation. They stopped for a few minutes and then started up once again. This time I was upset. Upset because they were fighting and also upset because they were being disobedient. I immediately got up to get a cane (yes – I'm a believer in spanking, as long as it doesn't lead to abuse). On this day however, I didn't have any intentions of spanking them – I'd been working on myself to find better ways to pass my message across to them, instead of yelling or spanking (unless, it was absolutely necessary). Yes! There are spank-worthy moments. I did want to get their attention and help them make a choice of squashing the squabble or getting spanked. I made it clear that I didn't want to know who was at fault and that they needed to learn to love each other and stop fighting. I take no glory in my approach, as I understand the journey of motherhood is one of learning and gets better over time. To keep the long story short, they chose to squash the fight. I guess neither of them liked the idea of being spanked.

God doesn't like it when we fight with people; in fact, He wants us to do our best to be at peace with everyone. While He recognizes we are human and disagreements are inevitable, if we all have the mindset of keeping the peace, not only will disagreements be minimized but when they do occur, they'll only be short-lived. *Now imagine how you'd feel as a parent if your kids rarely fought and instead showed love to each other most of the time?*

If it is possible, as far as it depends on you, live at peace with everyone.

—Romans 12:18 (NIV)

"Blessed are the peacemakers, for they shall be called sons of God."

—Matthew 5:9 (ESV)

Users Manual

We asked Sophie and Demi what they wanted for Christmas, and the list was long and changed frequently, but we noted a few items that seemed to remain on the list. The list ranged from toys to gadgets, and none sounded like books... haha, I wish. We had gotten them tablets a few years back, and they had literally destroyed them, perhaps they were too young to have them in the first place. My kids don't realize how fortunate they are to live in a time when having an electronic gadget – phone, tablet, etc. aren't completely unheard of and even having the opportunity to list out what they wanted for Christmas was an option.

I grew up in a household where Christmas gifts were not a thing – you didn't get asked what you wanted for Christmas nor did you get a Christmas gift. You were fortunate if you got a new outfit to be worn to church on Christmas Day. In fact, that was the only gift. I only found out about Christmas presents by watching TV and fantasizing about them. I guess that's why they are a big deal to me now. I don't want them to lack excitement over their presents; however, I'd be remiss if I didn't mention that I also don't want them to lose sight of the reason for the season, which is Jesus.

They didn't have iPads on their list this year – we had drummed it in their ears that since they didn't take care of their previous tablets, we wouldn't be replacing them, much less getting them iPads. The thrill in their voices and excitement in their faces when they got the iPads was priceless. They picked up the iPads, ignoring the manuals, and went straight to trying to turn them on . I asked them to wait and allow their dad to set them up first, before they started playing with them. A few days later, the iPads were configured and ready for use, but the user manuals were still in the box they came in, completely unused.

I recognize we are in the technology age, and they can probably get by using the iPads without much use for the user manual; however, if they were to take the time to go through the user manual, they are more likely to get more use out of it, figure out shortcuts, and probably give us a run for our money on their knowledge.

I liken the iPad user manual to the word of God. How many of us try to operate and run our lives without reading the Bible – which is in essence our user manual for how to live out our time on earth? How many times do we read it daily? How many times do we reference it to address issues of life? Have we read through the manual even just once in our lifetime? For those who have read it at least once, have we re-read to maximize what we get from it? Or are we only leveraging our basic potential, because we don't use the manual that is readily available to us? Food for thought.

All Scripture is breathed out by God and profitable for teaching, for reproof, for correction, and for training in righteousness, that the man of God may be complete, equipped for every good work.
—2 Timothy 3:16-17 (ESV)

Your word is a lamp to my feet and a light to my path.
—Psalm 119:105 (ESV)

Mummy

"Mummy!" Sophie shouted this a few times, and I responded each time with, "Yes, what can I do for you?" I didn't get a response, and she didn't show up at my door. Her room was only a few doors down from mine, and I could tell the difference between a "distressed" Mummy call and an "I need something" Mummy call. This was definitely an "I need something" Mummy call. I was expecting her to show up at my door and let me know what she wanted. However, since she didn't show up, I took that to mean what she wanted wasn't important enough to her to come find me. Being one of African descent, respect is a big part of our culture. Typically, if you want something from an adult, you go to them and ask; you don't summon them to you and then ask them for what you want. Scenarios that warrant the adult going to the child are when there is an emergency – e.g. the child fell down, needs help, etc.

Do you ever call on God in prayer and ask for something only once? Do you approach Him the right way or summon Him to attend to your need? It's very possible that once is all it takes to get an answer to the prayer. But when one time isn't enough, do you continue asking God or do you just keep waiting for an answer since you've asked once? If it's the latter, you may be waiting forever. Similar to my response or lack thereof to Sophie's call, God may be waiting on you to make the next move – ask more, ask more intently to show you're serious about your request, or perhaps use a different approach.

That you do not become sluggish, but imitate those who through faith and patience inherit the promises.
—Hebrews 6:12 (NKJV)

Then He spoke a parable to them, that men always ought to pray and not lose heart.
—Luke 18:1 (NKJV)

Excuses, Excuses, Excuses

Anyone who knows Sophie knows she has a voice, a voice she doesn't hesitate to use. She can talk up a storm if allowed. One of her habits is also making excuses when corrected. Instead of reflecting when given feedback, she always feels the need to explain herself. It doesn't matter what the feedback is because she is quick on her feet, she always has a come back ready. Initially, it was cute, until it wasn't. Her dad and I started correcting her and telling her to learn to listen more, talk less, and not always have an excuse for everything. I had just had one of these talks with her as she was making yet another excuse about why she hadn't done her homework. The conversation left me frustrated and wondering when we'd stop having this conversation repeatedly about not making excuses.

Little did I know that the lesson for the day was for me, yes, me! I was in the car with my husband, and he was giving me feedback about some food I had made. Without giving it much thought, I found myself explaining my reasons for why it was too salty and what not. And then the little voice popped in my head, reminding me of my conversation with Sophie earlier. It was glaring to me that the lesson wasn't just for her, but for me also. The saying about when you point a finger at a person, there are four more pointed at you was evident that day. You see it was such a simple incidence, but it really made me realize that I too had the habit of making excuses. *Do you do the same? Do you make excuses, instead of taking criticism?* What a moment of self-reflection this was for me. I also realized how much it displeases God when we don't learn from our shortcomings, but instead chose to make excuses. The good news is that since habits are formed, they can also be broken.

"But they all alike began to make excuses. The first one said to him, 'I have bought a piece of land and I need to go out and look at it; please consider me excused.'" Another one said, 'I have bought five yoke of oxen, and I am going to try them out; please consider me excused.'"
—Luke 14:18-19 (NASB)

"Who told you that you were naked?" the Lord God asked. "Have you eaten from the tree whose fruit I commanded you not to eat?" The man replied, "It was the woman you gave me who gave me the fruit, and I ate it." Then the Lord God asked the woman, "What have you done?" "The serpent deceived me," she replied. "That's why I ate it."
—Genesis 3:11-13 (NLT)

Right Focus

Sophie and Demi had a fundraiser at their school. They were raising funds for a little girl named Alexa who had a hole in her heart. When Sophie told me about the cause for the fundraiser, I was immediately touched and figured we would target raising the highest suggested amount per child which was $1,000. I wasn't sure how we were going to go about doing it, but figured with the right focus, prayer, and support, we would accomplish the goal. I wasn't aware that Demi was also supposed to raise funds so when I got a note in his school folder and he mentioned it to me a couple of days after Sophie's, I was surprised and even contemplated not doing it or reducing Sophie's goal. I figured we'd be reaching out to the same people and thought it'd be odd managing two campaigns. I thought about the fact that the goal was to raise funds for Alexa and decided targeting a smaller goal was better than not doing it at all. We set a goal of $250 for Demi.

When setting up Sophie's campaign, I found there were gifts for each milestone attained and a gift for any child who raised $1,000 or more. I figured the gifts were an added bonus to getting money for Alexa's treatment. We started sending out messages to family and friends, seeking their support in contributing funds towards the fundraiser. We recorded a video of Sophie where she told people about the cause and why they should donate. We had to shoot the short video a few times, because in the first two takes, Sophie spoke about the cause and also the gifts she would receive by meeting her goal. I told her that the gifts were an added bonus, but the focus was about the little girl who had a hole in her heart. I understood that as a child, the gifts were a big deal to her, but I didn't want her to lose sight of the most important aspect of the fundraiser. I reminded her of this each time she mentioned the gifts when she reached each milestone.

I learned through this that God blesses us when we are obedient to His word and will; however, the blessings aren't the main show or focus, doing God's will is. A lot of us, not excluding myself, tend to lose sight of what's important and focus on God's gifts or blessings instead of placing the focus on God Himself. The truth is that when we focus on God, the gifts and blessings are inevitable, but when we focus on the gifts and blessings instead of God, we stand the chance of losing sight of God. If Sophie focused on the gifts and included that message in her videos, I dare to say the support she received would have been minimal. I'm glad to say that she not only reached her goal, but exceeded it – additional lessons on this will be covered in a separate chapter. More importantly, we were excited that more money than we expected was raised for Alexa.

Therefore, since we are surrounded by such a great cloud of witnesses, let us throw off everything that hinders and the sin that so easily entangles. And let us run with perseverance the race marked out for us, fixing our eyes on Jesus, the pioneer and perfecter of faith. For the joy set before him he endured the cross, scorning its shame, and sat down at the right hand of the throne of God.

—Hebrews 12:1-2 (NIV)

Balance

I enjoy spending time with Sophie and Demi, and they enjoy spending time with me as well. There are times when we spend time with each other, when I want my space or feel like they are being clingy. It's in times like this that I appreciate and crave balance. Balance according to the dictionary means a condition in which different elements are equal or in the correct proportions. While spending time with each other is great, it needs to be done in the right proportion like anything else. I don't want them growing up without the right social skills or being awkwardly clingy. I want them to be able to spend quality time with me, and also enjoy time by themselves and with friends. Clinginess tends to exude timidity, and I'd rather them exude confidence and a level of independence.

I enjoy spending time with God, primarily because of the serenity it brings to me. I imagine God also enjoys me spending time with Him. However, He doesn't expect me to spend all my time with Him and not spend time with my family and siblings (both my own blood and spiritual siblings through Christ). He expects us to balance our time. Put Him first, spend time with Him, but also spend time fellowshipping with other humans. Imagine if I enjoyed spending time with God so much that I didn't spend time with my family, go to church, or spend time with my co-workers, etc. In no time, I'll likely be on the streets without a family, job, or church, unless I sobered up and added balance to my life. Like the saying goes, "Too much of anything is bad."

For God has not given us a spirit of timidity, but of power and love and discipline.

—2 Timothy 1:7 (NASB)

A false balance is an abomination to the Lord, but a just weight is his delight.

—Proverbs 11:1 (ESV)

iPad Update

I have found that it is possible to learn multiple lessons through the same incident, experience, tool, etc. This time, we're back to the iPad again. Isn't it interesting the lessons we can learn from seemingly little or trivial experiences? Demi and Sophie tend to ask their dad or I before downloading new games. More times than not, the answer is no. This response is for various reasons – sometimes, it's just bad timing when they ask; other times, it's because we feel they already have enough games downloaded or that they need to spend their time with more productive activities. One Sunday morning, Demi wanted to download a game, and because we had set restrictions that didn't allow him downloads without our approval, he asked as usual. The answer was no because trying to download a game while we were getting ready and almost running late for church wasn't ideal. I didn't stop him from using his iPad because he was already dressed for church. It turned out that while he was whining about not being allowed to download the game, he had unknowingly selected options to trigger a pending update. Anyone familiar with software updates knows it tends to take a while, especially when you're waiting for it to be completed. It feels like watching water boil. For him, the timing of this was frustrating, and the process seemed to take forever. His whining quickly shifted from the fact that he wasn't allowed to download the game to the fact that the software update was taking forever.

While he was complaining, Sophie said to him, "Why did you choose to complete the update? I always dismiss it. You're only supposed to update it once a year." She said this in her typical confident tone that'll leave anyone believing her if they didn't know any better. I immediately interrupted and said, "You should update it when the notifications come up because they address bugs and sometimes include enhancements." I see updates similar to a car tune up, regular doctors check-up visits, or dental cleaning. To me, they are a quick fix to address minor issues and ensure there are no bigger issues looming.

I strongly believe that God expects us to update ourselves from time to time. We should never remain stagnant in life. The update could look different for each of us; it could be taking a class to enhance our skills, updating our resume to prep for a new job, studying God's word, ensuring our doctor and dental visits are done at the right time. We shouldn't delay these updates for too long, or we could end up with bigger issues that would have been better managed when they were minor.

Do not be conformed to this world, but be transformed by the renewal of your mind, that by testing you may discern what is the will of God, what is good and acceptable and perfect.
—Romans 12:2 (ESV)

A good man leaves an inheritance to his children's children, but the sinner's wealth is laid up for the righteous.
—Proverbs 13:22 (ESV)

Tic Tac Toe

Valentine's Day seems to have taken a different turn from what it meant to me when I was growing up. During my teenage years, it started off with watching my older sister get excited about who would be her valentine for the year and what gifts she would get or would need to buy for the guy she had a thing for at the time. These days, it seems to have a different meaning depending on who you're talking to. For kids, it's about candy and getting stuff for their friends at school. For teenagers, it's about their crushes and what gifts they got or didn't get; for married couples, it's about rekindling love or showing extra affection. Recently, Sophie and Demi each purchased small tokens for each of their classmates and came home with bags filled with candy. I must mention I'm thankful for those parents who got pencils for their kids to give instead of candy. I've taken note of that for next year.

One of the goodies Sophie brought home was a valentine's themed tic tac toe game. She was excited about us playing. I played the first couple games with her and then she asked Demi to play with her. I wanted to make sure he understood the game before playing, so they could play a fair game. They both claimed he understood the game, until Demi played and it was apparent he didn't understand the rules of the game or that he needed to strategize his play in order to have a chance of winning. Let's just say that by the time the first game was over Demi was throwing a tantrum, upset that he didn't win, and started walking away. I wanted him to learn the game, but also to learn to fail upwards and not be a sore loser. I asked him to come back and try again, and this time I wanted to teach him how to play. Demi, still upset, said to me, "I'm never going to be good at it." Now learning how to play tic tac toe won't make a dent in his future, but those words hurt to hear. It wasn't the first time Demi had made such a comment when he was upset, and each time, he'd be corrected to speak positively and instead say the opposite – in this case, "I'll learn how to play and will be good at it."

I've heard people over time talk about speaking positively and not being negative, and for some reason, hearing Demi speak negatively made me take a deeper look at how God must feel when we say negative things or doubt that we can do something when all we need to do is take the time to learn the skill, game, or anything else. The first step to achieving this is believing we can. God is our cheerleader; He has even told us that we can do all things through His strength. This strength can come through inspiration, giving us the ability to learn, putting people in our paths to help or teach us, and the list goes on. Let's focus on speaking positively and not giving up before we even give ourselves a chance.

I can do all things through him who strengthens me.
—Philippians 4:13 (ESV)

And God is able to make all grace abound to you, so that having all sufficiency in all things at all times, you may abound in every good work.
—2 Corinthians 9:8 (ESV)

Another
Valentine's Day Saga

The tic tac toe game wasn't the only teachable experience we had on Valentine's Day. Earlier that day, after Sophie and Demi got back from school, they emptied their goody bags, exchanged some of their candy, and settled in for the day. I had taken the day off work and was in my room trying to get some rest. I had asked them to bring their homework, so I could look through and have them begin working on it. Sophie came into my room with a plate that had red things on it. I immediately figured it was something related to Valentine's Day, and I wasn't far from the truth. She had cut up some strawberries, some in half and others into very little bits. I was amazed at her thoughtfulness, gave her a kiss, and told her I'd eat it later. I happened to be fasting that day, and it wasn't time for me to break my fast.

She hopped on my bed, started telling me about her day, and then asked if she could have some of the strawberries. I didn't mind at all and said yes gladly. She had a few pieces, all the while telling me about her day as she popped each one in her mouth. I noticed the pieces were quickly diminishing as she absent mindedly popped each one in her mouth. Before I knew it, they were all gone. I stared at her in astonishment and said "I thought you made them for me? I asked you to eat some but didn't expect you to eat them all." Honestly at this point, I was slightly upset – not because I really wanted to eat the strawberries, I could easily have gotten some for myself later, but because she had offered them to me and then basically taken them back. One little thing she could have done to change my reaction was to ask if she could have it all and given me the chance to say yes or no.

I thought to myself: this is how God must feel when we promise Him something, get Him excited, and then do not fulfill our promises. I know God knows the full picture and is never surprised by our actions, but this doesn't eliminate the momentary feelings of disappointment or anger completely. The Bible is full of stories where God was angry with His children for doing one thing or the other; even though, it's not like He was unaware they were going to do it. In short, awareness doesn't remove the hurt. The next time you are about to commit or make a promise to God give it a second and third thought, and if there's a chance you won't be able to fulfil it, try not to make the commitment. On the flip side, if you've already made the commitment or promise, do all you can, including asking for God's assistance, in fulfilling it. He'll gladly assist you rather than watch you break the promise.

It is better not to promise anything than to promise something and not do it.

—Ecclesiastes 5:5 (NCV)

Commit to the LORD whatever you do, and he will establish your plans.

—Proverbs 16:3 (NIV)

Time and Season

Thumb sucking wasn't unfamiliar territory growing up. In fact, all six of my siblings plus my dad (as a child) were guilty of this at some point or the other. So when Sophie and Demi were born and they started sucking, I wasn't in the least bit surprised. Knowing firsthand how soothing and enjoyable sucking can be, my dilemma was whether or not to join family and friends when they tried to stop them from sucking or to leave them and allow them grow out of it with time. Sophie had pretty much stopped sucking by the time she was five; this, I believe, was in part due to when she was four my consistent message to her was that five year old's don't suck their thumbs. To my amazement, the trick worked, but she didn't stop cold turkey. By the time she was five, thumb sucking was down in frequency to a rarity. I wish I could say the same trick worked for Demi. He will be turning six soon, and I've since changed from telling him that five year old's don't suck, to telling him that six year old's don't suck.

I strongly believe there is a time and place for every-thing, and while persisting with thumb sucking when he is six is by no means the end of the world, the older he gets, the more repulsive it becomes. There are things we do that are cute when we are kids, but easily become a nuisance when we are grown and haven't let go of the habit. Imagine seeing a college student with no health challenges drinking milk out of a baby's bottle, or a man with per-fectly normal legs and limbs (along with no medical issues) crawling instead of walking. These examples may be far-fetched, but I hope they help in driving the point home. God sees everything we do, and He has appointed us at certain times or seasons to do things. Let's do our part in keeping with the proper time and season. One of my constant prayers is having the grace to do the right thing at the right time.

To everything there is a season, and a time to every purpose under heaven.

—Ecclesiastes 3:1 (ESV)

There is a time for everything, and a season for every activity under the heavens: a time to be born and a time to die, a time to plant and a time to uproot, a time to kill and a time to heal, a time to tear down and a time to build, a time to weep and a time to laugh, a time to mourn and a time to dance, a time to scatter stones and a time to gather them, a time to embrace and a time to refrain from embracing, a time to search and a time to give up, a time to keep and a time to throw away, a time to tear and a time to mend, a time to be silent and a time to speak, a time to love and a time to hate, a time for war and a time for peace.

—Ecclesiastes 3:1-8

Surrender

I've shared bits and pieces of my journey in deepening my relationship with God, which as you can tell, is still a work in progress. My ultimate goal is that these stories and lessons will aid in drawing you closer to God. I hope that you're now able to relate better with Him, as a child relates with a parent. Though we refer to God in the male tense, He is just as much a mother to us, as He is a father. Just as good parents yearn for relationships with their children, God yearns for relationships with us and just as no two parent-child relationships, even amongst siblings, are the same, don't expect your relationship with God to be the same as others. You have the ability to frame what your relationship with God is like, starting with an open mind, letting go of pre-set limits, and keeping in mind that the relationship is a process. With work, it will blossom over time.

If you've never given your life to Christ, talk about perfect timing. I can't think of a better time than now to begin a relationship with God. It's easy – say the following prayer, join a Bible and Christ-believing Church, and you'll be on your way to the journey of a lifetime. Prayer: *Lord Jesus, thank You for laying Your life that I may be saved. Today, I ask for forgiveness from every sin that has caused a limit in my ability to relate with You. Today, I ask that You become my Lord and personal Savior and that You grant me the grace to completely let go of my past mistakes and look on to a future with You. Thank You for loving and accepting me, in Jesus' name I pray. Amen.*

If you have given your life to Christ in the past but yearn for a recommitted relationship with Him, say the following prayer: Lord Jesus, thank You for saving me. I ask that You forgive me for every sin that has caused a break in our relationship. Today, I ask that You rekindle our relationship and make it better than I ever imagined. Help me to do my part in staying close to You through Your word in Jesus' name I pray, Amen.

About the Author

Lola Fadipe is proudly a daughter & an ambassador of the most-High God, who is in constant pursuit of a higher level of intimacy with the God. She is a child of Glory. She is a wife, mother of two children, Speaker, Mentor and Entrepreneur. Her purpose is to help people in whichever way she can, teaching lessons she has learned through personal experiences.